THE SENTIMENTAL 30'S

Project Manager: Tony Esposito
Cover Photo: © 1995 SUPERSTOCK VINTAGE, INC.

CONTENTS

GEORGIA ON MY MIND

Lyrics by
STUART GORRELL

Music by
HOAGY CARMICHAEL

Slowly

mf

p

F   A7   D7   D7 Aug   D7   G9   C7

Mel-o-dies bring mem-o-ries that lin-ger in my heart,_____

F   A Aug   A7   Dmi   G7   Edim   C9 7   F   C7 Aug

Make me think of Geor-gia, Why did we ev-er part?_____

F   A7   D7   D7 Aug   D7   G9   C7

Some sweet day when blos-soms fall and all the world's a song,_____

BETWEEN THE DEVIL AND THE DEEP BLUE SEA

Words by
TED KOEHLER

Music by
HAROLD ARLEN

what can I do? I don't know what makes me string a - long.

CHORUS

I don't want you, but I'd hate to lose you, You've got me

in be-tween the de-vil and the deep blue sea, I for-

give you, 'cause I can't for- get you, You've got me in be-tween the

de-vil and the deep blue sea, __ I ought to cross you off my list, __ but when you come knocking

at my door, __ Fate seems to give my heart a twist, and I come run-ning back for

more, I should hate you, but I guess I love you,

You've got me in be-tween __ the de-vil and the deep blue sea. __

LAZY RIVER

Words and Music by
HOAGY CARMICHAEL and SIDNEY ARODIN

I like la-zy weath er, I like la-zy days, Can't be blamed for hav-ing la - zy ways.

Some old la-zy riv - er sleeps be-side my door, Whis-p'ring to the sun – lit shore. —

From the Broadway Musical "SOPHISTICATED LADIES"

MOOD INDIGO

Words and Music by
DUKE ELLINGTON, IRVING MILLS
and ALBANY BIGARD

D.S. al Fine

WHEN THE MOON COMES OVER THE MOUNTAIN

Words and Music by
HARRY WOODS, HOWARD JOHNSON
and KATE SMITH

I'VE GOT THE WORLD ON A STRING

Words by
TED KOEHLER

Music by
HAROLD ARLEN

CHORUS

I've got the world on a string, ___ sit-tin' on a rain-bow, Got the string a-round my fin-

___ ger, What a world, what a life, ___ I'm in love! I've got a

song that I sing, ___ I can make the rain go, an-y time I move my fin - - ger,

Luck-y me, can't you see, I'm in love, ___ Life is a beau-ti-ful thing, ___

I DON'T STAND A GHOST OF A CHANCE
(With You)

Words by
BING CROSBY and
NED WASHINGTON

Music by
VICTOR YOUNG

I'M GETTIN' SENTIMENTAL OVER YOU

Words by
NED WASHINGTON

Music by
GEORGE BASSMAN

From the Metro-Goldwyn-Mayer Motion Picture "SHOOT THE MOON"

DON'T BLAME ME

Lyric by
DOROTHY FIELDS

Music by
JIMMY McHUGH

MARIA ELENA

English Lyrics by
S.K. RUSSELL

Music and Spanish Lyrics by
LORENZO BARCELATA

STARS FELL ON ALABAMA

Words by
MITCHELL PARISH

Music by
FRANK PERKINS

From the Broadway Musical Production "I MARRIED AN ANGEL"

SOPHISTICATED LADY

Words and Music by
DUKE ELLINGTON, IRVING MILLS
and MITCHELL PARISH

DEEP PURPLE
(Sombre Demijour)

Lyric by
MITCHELL PARISH

Music by
PETER DE ROSE

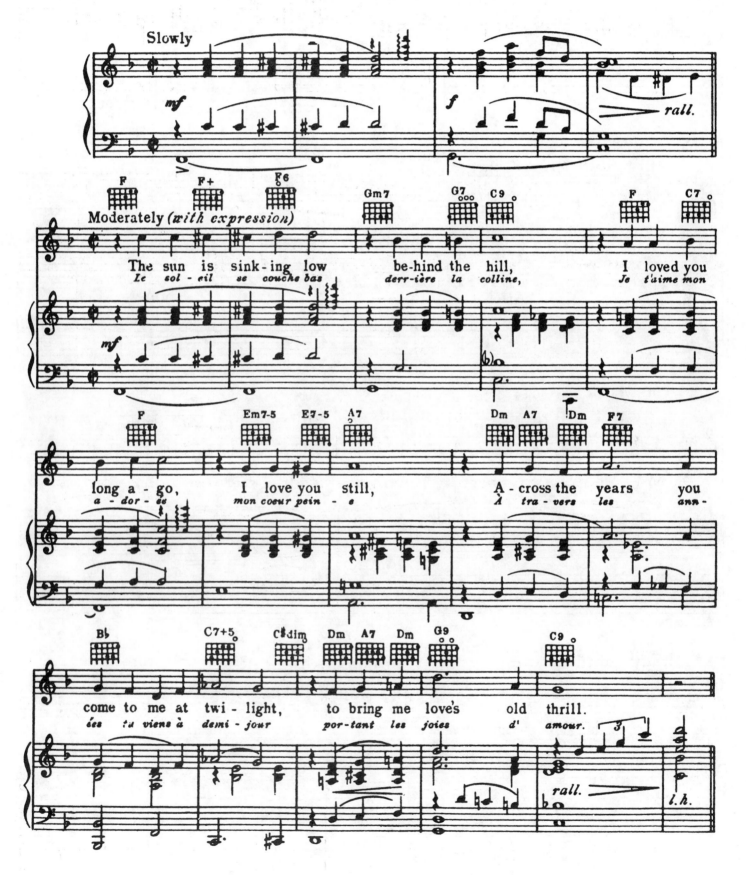

From the M-G-M Musical Production "WORDS AND MUSIC"

BLUE MOON

Lyrics by
LORENZ HART

Music by
RICHARD RODGERS

I'M IN THE MOOD FOR LOVE

Words and Music by
JIMMY McHUGH and
DOROTHY FIELDS

From the Motion Picture "SOME LIKE IT HOT"

STAIRWAY TO THE STARS

Words by
MITCHELL PARISH

Music by
MATT MALNECK and
FRANK SIGNORELLI

44

From the M-G-M Motion Picture "SAN FRANCISCO"

SAN FRANCISCO

Lyric by
GUS KAHN

Music by
BRONISLAU KAPER
and WALTER JURMANN

Moderately

San Fran - cis - co o - pen your gold - en gate

You let no stran - ger wait out - side your door___ San Fran -

- cis - co Here is your wan___ dering one say - ing "I'll wan - der no

more"_____ _____ Oth - er plac - es on - ly make me love you best Tell me you're the heart of all the gold - en west San Fran - cis - co wel - come me home____ a - gain I'm com - ing home_ to go roam - ing no more more____

STOMPIN' AT THE SAVOY

Lyric by
ANDY RAZAF

Music by
BENNY GOODMAN, CHICK WEBB
and EDGAR SAMPSON

ONCE IN A WHILE

Words by
BUD GREEN

Music by
MICHAEL EDWARDS

WHAT'S NEW?

Lyrics by
JOHNNY BURKE

Music by
BOB HAGGART

MOONLIGHT SERENADE

Words by
MITCHELL PARISH

Music by
GLENN MILLER

From the M-G-M Motion Picture "THE WIZARD OF OZ"

OVER THE RAINBOW

Lyric by
E. Y. HARBURG

Music by
HAROLD ARLEN

Dorothy - Judy Garland

YOU AND THE NIGHT AND THE MUSIC

Words by
HOWARD DIETZ

Music by
ARTHUR SCHWARTZ

Love like yours and mine Has the thrill-ing glow of spark-ling wine,

Make the most of time ere it has flown.____

REFRAIN (*Slowly, with much expression*)

You and the night and the mu-sic fill me with flam-ing de-

sire, Set-ting my be-ing com-plete-ly on

I GOT RHYTHM

Music and Lyrics by
GEORGE GERSHWIN
and IRA GERSHWIN

69

ABOUT A QUARTER TO NINE

Words by
AL DUBIN

Music by
HARRY WARREN

ZING! WENT THE STRINGS OF MY HEART

Words and Music by
JAMES F. HANLEY

75

TOO MARVELOUS FOR WORDS

Words by
JOHNNY MERCER

Music by
RICHARD A. WHITING

LULLABY OF BROADWAY

Words by
AL DUBIN

Music by
HARRY WARREN

Moderately fast

Come on a-long and lis-ten to___ the lul-la-by of Broad-way.

The hip hoo-ray and bal-ly-hoo,—
The hi-dee-hi and boop-a-doo,—
the lul-la-by of Broad-way.

The rum-ble of a sub-way train,___ the rat-tle of the tax-is.
The band be-gins to go to town,___ and ev-'ry one goes cra-zy.

The daf - fy-dils who en - ter - tain __ at An - ge - lo's and Max - ie's. When a
You rock - a - bye your ba - by 'round __ 'til ev - 'ry-thing gets ha - zy. Hush - a -

Broad - way ba - by says "Good night," it's ear - ly in the morn - ing.
bye, I'll buy you this and that," you hear a dad - dy say - ing.

Man-hat - tan ba - bies don't sleep tight __ un - til the dawn:
And ba - by goes home to her flat __ to sleep all day:

Good - night, Ba - by,

8va bassa ad lib -

WHO CARES?
(So Long As You Care For Me)

Music and Lyrics by
GEORGE GERSHWIN
and IRA GERSHWIN

Let it rain and thun-der! Let a mil-lion

firms go un-der! I am not con-cerned with

Stocks and bonds that I've been burned with._____ I love you and you love me And that's how it will al-ways be, And noth-ing else can ev-er mean a thing._____ Who cares what the pub-lic chat-ters?_____ Love's the on-ly thing that mat-ters._____ Who

Refrain
(in a lilting manner)

JEEPERS CREEPERS

Words by
JOHNNY MERCER

Music by
HARRY WARREN

I don't care what the weath-er man says, When the weath-er man says it's rain-ing, You'll nev-er hear me com-plain-ing, I'm cer-tain the sun will shine, I don't care how the

NIGHT AND DAY

French version by
EMELIA RENAUD

Words and Music by
COLE PORTER

Like the beat, beat, beat, of the tom-tom; When the jun - gle shad - ows
Com - me le rou - le - ment du tam - tam, Quand la jon - gle s'ob - scur -

fall, Like the tick, tick, tock of the state - ly clock, as it stands a - gainst the
cit, Com - me le tic - tac de l'hor - lo - ge ma - jes - tu - eu - se près du

wall, Like the drip, drip, drip, of the rain-drops, When the sum - mer show'r is
mur Com - me la gout - te d'eau qui tom - be Quand un o - rage est fi -

94

HOORAY FOR HOLLYWOOD

Words by
JOHNNY MERCER

Music by
RICHARD A. WHITING

HOO-RAY FOR HOL-LY-WOOD!_____ That screw-y
That phon-y

bal-ly-hoo-ey Hol-ly-wood,_____ Where an-y
su-per Con-ey Hol-ly-wood,_____ They come from

BEGIN THE BEGUINE

Words and Music by
COLE PORTER

Spanish Version by
MARIA GREVER

I ONLY HAVE EYES FOR YOU

Words by
AL DUBIN

Music by
HARRY WARREN

THE GOLD DIGGERS' SONG
(WE'RE IN THE MONEY)

Words by
AL DUBIN

Music by
HARRY WARREN

FORTY-SECOND STREET

Words by
AL DUBIN

Music by
HARRY WARREN

SOMETHING TO REMEMBER YOU BY

Words by
HOWARD DIETZ

Music by
ARTHUR SCHWARTZ

You are leav-ing me, and I will try to face the world a - lone. What will be will be, but time can-not e - rase the love we've known.

ANYTHING GOES

Words and Music by
COLE PORTER

YOU GO TO MY HEAD

Words by
HAVEN GILLESPIE

Music by
J. FRED COOTS

AS TIME GOES BY

Words and Music by
HERMAN HUPFELD

FINE AND DANDY

Words by
PAUL JAMES

Music by
KAY SWIFT

AUTUMN IN NEW YORK

Words and Music by
VERNON DUKE

Andantino *(poco rubato)*

mp

Gm   C7   F

p

It's time to end my lone-ly hol-i-day___ And bid the

poco rit.   *p legato*

C7   Fm   C   Gm   C7

coun-try a has-ty fare - well.   So on this gray and mel-an-

138

BROTHER, CAN YOU SPARE A DIME?

Words by
E.Y. HARBURG

Music by
JAY GORNEY

JUST ONE OF THOSE THINGS

Words and Music by
COLE PORTER

"Don't for-get to drop a line to me, please," As Jul-iet cried

in her Ro-meo's ear, "Ro - meo, why not face the fact, my dear?"

REFRAIN

It was just one of those things, Just one

of those cra-zy flings. One of those bells that now and then rings,

IT'S ONLY A PAPER MOON

Words by
BILLY ROSE and E.Y. HARBURG

Music by
HAROLD ARLEN

YOU'RE GETTING TO BE A HABIT WITH ME

Words by
AL DUBIN

Music by
HARRY WARREN

BODY AND SOUL

Words by
EDWARD HEYMAN, ROBERT SOUR
and FRANK EYTON

Music by
JOHN GREEN